RAMBLING BOOTS PUBLISHING

Get Your Side Hustle Hustling

In 6 Easy Steps

First edition

This book was professionally typeset on Reedsy.
Find out more at reedsy.com

This Is Dedicated To My Inner Circle
I'm Forever Grateful for All
The Love and Support through My Journey

Contents

Introduction

Many things have changed with the turn of the century as they always do. The way people make a living is no exception. Prior generations were taught that hard work would lead to success with enough time put in. Retirement was the ultimate end goal and it would take years to get there. If you couldn't make ends meet then you needed to get a second or third job or make a budget and live below your means.

Some people took this idea and ran with it for as long as their bodies would let them. Others took this idea and tossed it out with Monday's trash the moment their hobby began to generate enough income to pay the bills. They found that doing what they loved alongside being their own boss provided more rewards and happiness than the job their college education could offer.

However, the rest of us who tried to follow our dreams and find the perfect side hustle that could fill our bank accounts and allow time off, found that the side hustle was not as easy as it looked.

In time, we had to look for full-time day jobs (or in my case night jobs) just to make ends meet. This course of action left our once passion-filled dream of having our own business for doing what we loved in the closet behind the corporate uniform.

Fortunately, in recent years, a new understanding of the side hustle

1

has evolved from a fringe idea to a mainstream phenomenon. Once again, people began adding to their nine-to-five jobs with passion projects, freelance gigs, and entrepreneurial ventures. There has been an explosion of opportunities with advancing technology. People are trying once more to build a main hustle from their side hustle.

These new opportunities have brought along their share of challenges. As the world of side hustles continues to evolve, the pressure to stand out and succeed can be overwhelming. If you've recently embarked on your own side hustle and find yourself needing a fresh perspective to push it towards success, you're certainly not alone. Many entrepreneurs are facing similar struggles, whether it's finding the right niche, reaching their target audience, or maintaining motivation amidst the constant demands of their primary job and personal life. This journey can be isolating, but it's important to remember that others are navigating the same hurdles. The key lies in recognizing these challenges as stepping stones rather than roadblocks, and in seeking out new strategies, tools, and communities that can help you refine your approach and sustain your momentum.

But starting a side hustle is only the beginning. Many find that maintaining momentum and achieving success is where the real challenge lies. The personal sacrifice of effort to find progress can be difficult. Let's uncover why people often abandon their side hustles, from burnout and lack of direction to unforeseen obstacles and shifting priorities. By understanding these pitfalls, you'll be better equipped to navigate them and avoid the devastation and heartbreak they can lead to.

In this book, you'll find practical strategies and actionable insights to help you start, sustain, and thrive in your side hustle. From setting realistic goals and managing time effectively to leveraging resources and staying motivated, each chapter is designed to provide the tools and knowledge to "Get your side hustle hustling" into a successful and profitable business.

Prepare to embark on a journey that will transform your approach to side hustles, offering you the guidance needed to turn your aspirations into achievements. Whether you're just starting or looking to reignite an existing business, this book is your road map to side hustle success.

1

Assessment of Your Side Hustle

E mbarking on a side hustle is an exciting journey filled with potential and promise. However, before diving headfirst into the multiple opportunities offered to you, it's crucial to take a step back and assess your motivations and readiness. Understanding why you're starting this business and evaluating your commitment can significantly impact your long-term success. This chapter will lead you through a thorough self-assessment to see if you are ready to align with your goals and aspirations.

Passion

Passion is a powerful driver behind many successful side hustles. Genuine excitement about your side hustle can sustain you through the challenges and setbacks that will inevitably arise. Ask yourself: What excites me about this business? If the answer revolves around a deep-seated interest or enthusiasm for the work itself, then you're on the right track. Passion fuels persistence and innovation, which are key essentials for overcoming obstacles and achieving success.

Consider how your side hustle aligns with your interests. Is it something you've always wanted to do or explore further? If your hustle allows you to channel your passions into productive and creative outlets, you're more likely to remain engaged and motivated. However, be cautious of mistaking excitement for a fleeting interest. Your passion must be strong enough to sustain you through the ups and downs.

Money

Financial gain is a common and practical motivation for starting a side hustle. It's important to assess whether your primary goal is to boost your income, save for a specific purpose, or achieve financial independence. Understand the implications of your side hustle, including startup costs, potential earnings, and time investment.

While money is a legitimate and essential motivator, it's crucial to balance it with other factors. Relying solely on financial incentives can lead to burnout if the work doesn't align with your interests or skills. Ensure that your financial goals are realistic and that your side hustle can provide a sustainable and satisfying income stream without compromising your overall well-being.

Skills

Utilizing your existing skills or developing new ones can be a significant motivator for starting a side hustle. Assess what unique abilities or expertise you bring to the table and how they can be leveraged in your favor. Can you begin with what you know today or will you need to learn something new? Can you hire someone to help with the required skills that you don't possess?

If your side hustle aligns with your skill set, it can enhance your efficiency and effectiveness. Moreover, it allows you to build on your strengths and potentially offer high-quality services or products. However, if you find that the side hustle requires skills you don't currently possess, consider whether you're willing and able to invest the time and effort to acquire them.

Hobbies

Turning a hobby into a side hustle can be a fulfilling way to monetize something you already love doing. If your side hustle is based on a personal interest or pastime, it can bring additional joy and satisfaction to your life. Decide whether this hobby has the potential to become a profitable and sustainable business.

However, be mindful of the potential risks of monetizing a hobby. Sometimes, turning something you love into a business can alter your perception of it and reduce the enjoyment you once derived from it. Consider whether you're comfortable with this shift and if you're prepared to approach your hobby with a business mindset.

Is This What You Want to do or Were You Told to do It?

External influences, such as advice from friends, family, or mentors, can sometimes motivate individuals to start a side hustle. While this external encouragement can be valuable, it's important to assess whether the idea belongs to you or someone else. Reflect on why you're pursuing this particular interest. Is it because you believe in it or simply because someone suggested it?

Being motivated by external pressures can lead to a lack of personal commitment and passion. Ensure that your side hustle aligns with your personal interests and goals, rather than being solely influenced by others' expectations or opinions.

Challenge vs. Boredom

Evaluate whether your side hustle idea challenges and excites you or if it feels mundane and uninspiring. A successful side hustle should provide a sense of accomplishment and growth. If the prospect of working on this venture excites you and pushes you to grow, it's a positive sign. Conversely, if you find the idea unchallenging or boring, it might not be the right fit for you.

Ask yourself: Does this side hustle stimulate my creativity and problem-solving abilities, or does it feel like a tedious task? Engaging with a challenging and stimulating project can enhance your motivation and drive, whereas boredom can lead to a lack of motivation and put your side hustle on a side table.

Is There A Desire to Continue?

Finally, consider your long-term commitment to the side hustle. Reflect on whether you see yourself continuing with it into the future. Assess your willingness to invest time, effort, and resources into it, even when faced with obstacles or slower-than-expected progress.

Ask yourself: Am I prepared to stay committed to this side hustle, and do I envision it growing into something significant? Can you see a clear vision and readiness for ongoing dedication that can help you overcome challenges and build a successful and sustainable business?

Assessing your motivations and readiness is a critical first step in starting a successful side hustle. By understanding what drives you—whether it's passion, financial gain, skills, hobbies, external influences, or the challenge—it becomes easier to align your efforts with your goals. This self-assessment will not only clarify your intentions but also prepare you for the journey ahead.

In the chapters that follow, we'll delve deeper into how to leverage these motivations to set realistic goals, develop a structured plan, and address common challenges. With a solid foundation built on a clear understanding of your motivations, you'll be well-equipped to turn your side hustle into a rewarding and successful life achievement.

2

Revise the Business Plan

Starting a side hustle is an exciting opportunity, but to make it triumphant, you need a well-thought-out business plan. This chapter will guide you through the essential components of creating a plan that works for you. Your business will not only thrive, but it will stand to triumph over devastating challenges and give victory to your sacrifices.

What Worked - Focus on What You Enjoy Doing

The first step in developing a successful business plan is to evaluate what has worked well so far. Consider the aspects of your side hustle that you genuinely enjoy. What tasks or activities have brought you the most satisfaction? Whether it's creating the product, interacting with customers, or managing your finances, identifying what you love doing will help you stay motivated and focused. The parts of your side hustle that you enjoy are likely the ones where you excel, so prioritize these elements in your plan.

What Didn't Work - Find Help for the Weak Links

Just as important as knowing what works is recognizing what doesn't. Are there tasks you dread or struggle with? If so, it's time to find help. You don't have to do everything alone. Consider outsourcing tasks that you find difficult or time-consuming. For example, if you're not great at marketing, hire someone who is. If bookkeeping isn't your strength, find an accountant. Delegating these tasks allows you to focus on the areas where you excel and makes certain that every aspect of your business is handled by someone who knows what they're doing.

What Can You Improve?

No business is perfect, and there's always room for improvement. In your business plan, outline the areas where you can make enhancements. This could be in your product, skill set, inventory management, or time management.

Product or Service Quality

Consider whether your product or service meets the needs of your target audience. Are there ways to improve quality, design, or functionality? Customer feedback can be invaluable here. Regularly evaluate its quality, design, and functionality to ensure it meets or exceeds the expectations of your target audience. Ask yourself: Is your product or service meeting customer needs? Are there features or aspects that could be refined? Collecting feedback from customers can provide valuable insights. Listen to their suggestions and complaints, and be willing to make necessary adjustments.

Skill

As the owner of your side hustle, your skills are one of your most

REVISE THE BUSINESS PLAN

valuable assets. Are there areas where you could benefit from additional training or education? Investing in your skill development can lead to better products, more efficient processes, and ultimately, a more successful business. Identify areas where you can expand or sharpen your expertise. Consider new trends or techniques in your industry that you need to learn. Is training or certifications available that benefit your business? Whether it's taking a course, attending workshops, or seeking mentorship, enhancing your skills will give you a competitive edge and boost your confidence.

Inventory

If your side hustle involves selling physical products, managing your inventory is crucial. Make certain that you have enough stock to meet demand without overstocking, which can tie up your capital. Consider using inventory management software to keep track of your stock levels and streamline your operations. Knowing what you have in stock will give you the ability to know what you need to replenish or get rid of to encourage rising profits.

Realistic Time Commitment

Time is one of the most valuable resources for entrepreneurs. Effective time management can have incredible effects on your business plan, so it's essential to outline a realistic time commitment for your business. Consider how much time you can realistically dedicate to your side hustle on a daily, weekly, and monthly basis. Start by assessing your current schedule. What other commitments do you have, and how much time do they require? Look at how much time you spend in certain areas of your business. If you find an area taking more time than you have then look for ways to improve it. This could mean hiring someone to help or delegating small tasks. If you are spending too much time in an area that is not profitable then look at ways to reallocate it to something that is more profitable. Be realistic about what you can accomplish in the time you have. It's better to set modest goals and exceed them than to over-commit and burn out. Remember that consistency is key. Even if you can only dedicate a few hours a week to your side hustle, make sure those hours are productive and focused. This allows you to concentrate on high-impact activities that drive growth.

Do You Have the Right Resources & Enough of Them to Be Efficient?

Efficiency is the ability to reach your goal with little waste of effort or energy. It is critical for the life of your side hustle. In your business plan, evaluate whether you have the right resources to operate efficiently. This includes everything from the tools and equipment you need to the people who can support you. Do you have the necessary software, technology, or supplies to run your business smoothly? If not, consider investing in the resources that will make your operations more efficient. Additionally, assess whether you have enough of these resources to meet demand. Running out of stock, for example, can lead to missed sales opportunities and dissatisfied customers. Also, consider the human resources willing to help. Do you have a network of people you can rely on for advice, support, or collaboration? Building a team, even if it's just a few trusted advisors, can significantly boost your effort.

Find the aspects of your side hustle that align with your strengths. Prioritizing these areas will keep you motivated and focused, creating a road map for ongoing growth to better outcomes. Acknowledge tasks that you can eliminate to enhance your business's overall efficiency and effectiveness. Set achievable goals based on your schedule to maintain consistency and avoid burnout. Secure enough resources to meet demand and maintain smooth operations. Execute changes that not only overcome current challenges but position your side hustle to adapt and expand in a competitive market. This structured approach will help you build and implement a business plan with stability and make your side hustle victorious.

3

Make Goals and Clear Visions

With a solid business plan in place, the next step is to set clear goals for your side hustle. This chapter will guide you through the process of defining your target market, understanding your competitors, and setting realistic goals that will help you achieve long-term success.

Who is Your Target Market?

Understanding your target market is crucial to the success of your side hustle. Who are you trying to reach with your product or service? Consider the demographics, interests, and needs of your ideal customer. The more specific you can be, the better. Once you've defined your target market, tailor your marketing and sales strategies to appeal directly to them. This might involve creating targeted advertisements, developing content that resonates with their interests, or offering promotions that meet their needs.

Competitors

Knowing who your competitors are and what they offer is essential for staying competitive. Research other businesses in your niche to understand what they're doing well and where there might be gaps in the market. Analyze their pricing, marketing strategies, and customer service. How does your side hustle compare? Use this information to differentiate yourself and offer something unique that sets you apart from the competition.

Is the Quality Good Enough to Sell to Your Grandma?

A simple yet effective way to evaluate your product or service is to ask yourself: Is it good enough to sell to your grandma? In other words, is it of a quality that you would confidently offer to someone you care about? High-quality products and services are more likely to generate positive reviews, repeat business, and word-of-mouth referrals. If you're not confident in the quality of what you're offering, take steps to improve it before promoting your side hustle.

Plan Short-term Goal Wins and Make Long-Term Goals

Setting goals is an essential part of any successful side hustle. Start by identifying short-term goals that are realistic and achievable. These "quick wins" can help build momentum and keep you motivated. For example, your short-term goals might include securing your first few customers, launching your website, or reaching a specific sales target. In addition to short-term goals, it's crucial to set long-term goals that align with your vision for the future. What do you want your side hustle to look like in one, three, or five years? These long-term goals should be ambitious but attainable with consistent effort and dedication.

Use Baby Steps to Reach Long-Term Goals

Achieving long-term goals can be daunting, but breaking them down into smaller, manageable steps can make them more attainable. Identify the baby steps that will move you closer to your long-term vision. For example, if your long-term goal is to build a sustainable online business, your baby steps might include developing a content marketing strategy, building an email list, and increasing your social media presence. Each small step you take will bring you closer to your ultimate goal, making the process feel less overwhelming and more achievable.

Long-Term Vision: Sustainable Growth and Success

Your side hustle's success hinges on your ability to plan for sustainable growth. This means not only focusing on immediate profits but also building a business that can thrive in the long term. Consider what sustainable growth looks like for your side hustle. This might involve expanding your product line, entering new markets, or increasing your customer base. Whatever your vision, make sure your goals and strategies align with achieving long-term success.

4

Customers and Pricing

O nce you have a clear business plan and set goals, the next step is to effectively market your side hustle and price your offerings competitively. This chapter will explore how to reach your target audience, ensure your customers have a positive experience, and develop a pricing strategy that works.

Is There a Platform to Reach the Target Audience?

To effectively market your side hustle, you need to be where your target audience is. Identify the platforms where your potential customers spend their time. This might include social media sites, online forums, or specific industry websites. Once you've identified these platforms, focus on creating content and advertisements that resonate with your target audience. Tailor your messaging to address their needs, desires, and interests. The more effectively you can reach your target audience, the more successful your marketing efforts will be.

Are You Reaching the Intended Target?

It's not enough to simply be present on the right platforms; you also need to ensure that your message is reaching the right people. Monitor your marketing efforts to see if you're attracting your intended target audience. Use analytics tools to track who is engaging with your content and whether they fit your target demographic. If you're not reaching the right people, adjust your strategy. This might involve refining your messaging, targeting different keywords, or using more specific targeting options in your ads.

Can Customers See Reviews and Leave Reviews?

Customer reviews are a powerful tool for building trust and credibility. Make sure your customers can easily see reviews from others and leave their own. Encourage satisfied customers to share their experiences, and respond promptly to any negative feedback. Positive reviews can significantly influence potential customers' purchasing decisions, so prioritize providing excellent service and asking for reviews.

Can Customers Get Good Customer Service?

Good customer service is crucial for retaining customers and generating positive word-of-mouth. Ensure that your customers can easily contact you with questions or concerns and that you're responsive to their needs. Consider offering multiple channels for customer support, such as email, phone, and live chat. Offering self-service options like a detailed FAQ page or tutorial videos can also be beneficial, helping customers find the information they need without having to reach out directly. The better your customer service, the more likely customers are to return and recommend your business to others.

Providing excellent customer service is crucial for the success of your side hustle. No matter how great your advertising is, poor customer service can quickly turn potential customers away.

Good customer service is not just about responding to inquiries—it's about creating a positive experience that encourages repeat business and word-of-mouth referrals. Investing time in providing quality service can turn one-time buyers into loyal customers who help grow your side hustle.

Are the Details Complete for your Product or Service?

When marketing your product or service, it's essential to provide complete and accurate details. Customers need to know exactly what they're getting, including specifications, features, and benefits. Clear, concise descriptions help build trust and prevent misunderstandings. Make sure all the information about your product or service is readily available on your website, product pages, and marketing materials. The more transparent you are, the more confident customers will feel about making a purchase.

When customers look at your ads or visit your online store, they need to find all the necessary information to make a purchase decision. Incomplete or vague descriptions can lead to confusion and lost sales.

Make sure your product or service descriptions are thorough and clear, covering all key aspects like features, benefits, pricing, and how to use the product. High-quality images or videos that showcase your offerings from different angles can also enhance the customer's experience.

Transparency is expected. Be upfront about any additional costs, such as shipping or service fees, and provide clear return and refund policies. This helps build trust with your customers and reduces the chances of dissatisfaction after the purchase.

Does the Price Make Sense for Your Target Audience?

Pricing is a main priority for your customers and the life of your business. It not only affects your profits but also influences how customers perceive your product or service. Your price needs to align with your target audience's expectations and what they're willing to pay.

Understanding the financial background and spending habits of your target audience is key to setting the right price. For example, a high-end product might not appeal to a budget-conscious audience, while a lower-priced item might be seen as low quality by those willing to spend more.

Competitor analysis is also important. Knowing what others in your niche are charging can help you position your pricing effectively. Additionally, consider psychological pricing strategies, such as charm pricing (e.g., $9.99 instead of $10) or offering multiple price points, to make your pricing more appealing.

What Are Your Pricing Strategies?

There are several pricing strategies you can use depending on your side hustle's goals and the nature of your product or service. Some common strategies include:

*Cost-Plus Pricing: This involves adding a markup to the cost of producing your product. It's straightforward but doesn't take into account market demand or competition.

*Value-Based Pricing: Setting your price based on the perceived value to the customer rather than the cost. This requires a deep understanding of what your customers value and are willing to pay for.

*Penetration Pricing: Offering a low price when you first enter the market to attract customers and build a base. You can then gradually increase the price as you establish your brand.

*Skimming Pricing: Starting with a high price to maximize profits from early adopters, then lowering the price over time to reach more price-sensitive customers.

*Dynamic Pricing: Adjusting your prices based on demand, competition, and other factors. This is common in industries like e-commerce and travel.

Choosing the right pricing strategy involves considering market conditions, your target audience's behavior, and your overall business goals. Experimenting with different strategies and analyzing their impact can help you find the most effective approach.

Customer service and pricing are vital components to the profits of side hustle. By choosing the right platforms, targeting the correct audience, ensuring clear communication, and selecting appropriate pricing strategies, you can create a compelling value proposition that resonates with your customers. As you grow your side hustle, regularly refining these elements will be key to sustaining and expanding your goals.

5

Avoid Common Mistakes

S tarting and maintaining a side hustle can be an incredibly rewarding experience, but it also comes with its own set of challenges. In this chapter, we'll explore some of the most common mistakes that can hinder your progress and how to avoid them.

Procrastination

Procrastination is a common hurdle for many entrepreneurs, especially when juggling a side hustle alongside other responsibilities. It's easy to delay tasks, particularly those that seem daunting or tedious, but this can lead to missed opportunities and stalled progress.

To combat procrastination, it's essential to break tasks into smaller, manageable steps and set clear deadlines. Prioritizing tasks and using tools like to-do lists or project management apps can help keep you on track. Remember, consistent small efforts often lead to significant results over time.

Poor Time Management

While it's important to dedicate time to your side hustle, over-commitment can lead to burnout. Balancing your side hustle with other aspects of your life is crucial for maintaining your well-being and sustaining your business in the long run.

Set realistic boundaries for how much time you spend on your side hustle each week. This might mean taking time to enjoy something you love not related to your business. It's important to recognize when it's time to take a break and recharge. Maintaining a healthy work-life balance will help you stay motivated and productive.

Unrealistic Goals

Setting goals is vital for the growth of your side hustle, but unrealistic goals can lead to frustration and disappointment. It's easy to get carried away with grand visions of success, but setting attainable, short-term goals is more effective.

Start by setting SMART goals—Specific, Measurable, Achievable, Relevant, and Time-bound. This approach ensures that your goals are realistic and actionable, helping you stay focused and motivated. As you achieve these smaller goals, you can gradually set more ambitious targets, building momentum over time.

Losing Motivation and Interest

Maintaining motivation can be challenging, especially when progress is slow or when faced with setbacks. It's not uncommon to lose interest in your side hustle if it feels like it's not growing as expected.

To keep your motivation high, revisit your initial reasons for starting the side hustle. Remind yourself of the passion and excitement you had at the beginning. Regularly celebrating small wins and milestones can also help you stay positive and engaged. If you find yourself losing interest, it might be time to reassess your goals or pivot your approach to something that reignites your enthusiasm.

Feeling Overwhelmed

Running a side hustle can be overwhelming, especially when you're wearing multiple hats—marketer, accountant, product developer, and customer service rep all at once. The sheer volume of tasks can make it difficult to know where to start.

To manage this feeling that you're drowning, consider delegating or outsourcing tasks that are outside your expertise or that consume too much time. Breaking down larger projects into smaller tasks can also make them feel more manageable. Prioritizing your tasks by urgency and importance will help you focus on what truly matters, reducing stress and making your workload more manageable.

Poor Financial Decisions

Financial mismanagement is a common pitfall in running a side hustle. Whether it's underestimating expenses, overspending on unnecessary tools, or failing to save for taxes, poor financial decisions can quickly derail your business.

It's essential to keep a close eye on your finances from the start. Create a budget that outlines all your expenses and expected income. Regularly review your finances to ensure you're staying on track. Consider using accounting software to manage your finances more efficiently and consult with a financial advisor when necessary. Additionally, reinvesting a portion of your profits back into your side hustle can help fuel growth and long-term success.

Fear of Failure

Fear of failure is one of the biggest obstacles many side hustlers face. It can prevent you from taking necessary risks or even starting in the first place. However, failure is often a stepping stone to success, offering valuable lessons and opportunities for growth.

To overcome the fear of failure, view it as a learning opportunity rather than a negative outcome. Every setback provides insights that can improve your future efforts. Surround yourself with a supportive network of friends, family, or fellow entrepreneurs who can offer encouragement and perspective. Remember, the only true failure is not trying at all.

Avoiding these common mistakes can significantly increase your chances of success in your side hustle. By staying organized, setting realistic goals, managing your time and finances wisely, and maintaining a positive mindset, you can navigate the challenges of entrepreneurship and build a thriving business. As you move forward, remember that every challenge you face is an opportunity to learn, grow, and get closer to achieving your goals.

6

Surround Yourself with Like Minded People

Building a successful side hustle or small business requires not just hard work and dedication, but also the right support system. Surrounding yourself with like-minded individuals can provide the encouragement, guidance, and inspiration you need to stay motivated and achieve your goals. In this chapter, we'll explore how connecting with others who share your entrepreneurial spirit can make a significant difference in your journey.

Small Business Clubs

Joining small business clubs or associations can be incredibly beneficial for anyone looking to grow their side hustle. These groups bring together entrepreneurs who are facing similar challenges and opportunities, creating a space where you can share ideas, gain insights, and build valuable relationships.

Small business clubs often host networking events, workshops, and seminars that provide learning opportunities and help you stay informed about industry trends. Being part of such a community allows you to exchange knowledge, collaborate on projects, and even find potential partners or clients. The connections you make in these clubs can open doors to new opportunities and provide a strong support network as you navigate the ups and downs of entrepreneurship.

Support Groups

Entrepreneurship can be a lonely journey, especially when you're working on a side hustle in addition to other responsibilities. Support groups can offer a safe space to share your experiences, challenges, and victories with others who understand what you're going through.

These groups often focus on specific aspects of running a business, such as overcoming obstacles, managing stress, or achieving work-life balance. Being part of a support group can help you feel less isolated and provide practical advice on dealing with the emotional and psychological challenges of entrepreneurship. Moreover, the encouragement and accountability from group members can keep you motivated and focused on your goals.

Talk to Other Successful People in the Same Field

One of the best ways to learn and grow in your side hustle is by connecting with others who have already achieved success in your field. These individuals can offer valuable insights, share their experiences, and provide guidance to navigate through the challenges you may face.

Reach out to successful entrepreneurs in your industry, whether through networking events, social media, or mutual connections. Don't be afraid to ask for advice or mentorship—most successful people are happy to share their knowledge and help others on their journey.

Learning from their mistakes and successes can save you time and effort, helping you avoid common pitfalls and adopt strategies that work.

Success Stories

Reading or listening to success stories can be incredibly inspiring and motivating. They serve as a reminder that achieving your goals is possible, even when the road seems tough. Success stories highlight the perseverance, creativity, and resilience required to overcome obstacles and reach new heights in your business.

Look for success stories in books, podcasts, blogs, or within your network. Pay attention to the lessons these stories offer and think about how you can apply them to your personal journey. Success stories not only provide motivation but also practical insights that can help you refine your approach and stay committed to your vision.

Coaching

Working with a coach can be a game-changer for your business. A coach can provide personalized guidance, help you set and achieve goals, and offer an outside perspective on your business. They can also hold you accountable, ensuring that you stay on track and make consistent progress.

Coaching is particularly valuable when you're facing challenges or feel stuck in your business. A coach can help you identify the root causes of your struggles, develop strategies to overcome them and build the confidence you need to move forward. Whether you opt for one-on-one coaching or group coaching sessions, having a mentor who understands your journey can accelerate your growth and success.

Find Encouragement

Encouragement is crucial for sustaining motivation and pushing through difficult times. Surround yourself with people who believe in you and your vision—friends, family, mentors, or fellow entrepreneurs who can offer support when you need it most.

Encouragement doesn't just come from others; it can also come from within. Practice self-encouragement by celebrating small wins, acknowledging your progress, and staying positive even when faced with setbacks. Keeping a positive mindset and focusing on your achievements can help you maintain the momentum needed to reach your goals.

Focus on the Possibility of Succeeding, Not Failure

A key mindset shift that can make a significant difference in your entrepreneurial journey is focusing on the possibility of success rather than the fear of failure. It's natural to have doubts and worries, but dwelling on them can hinder your progress and prevent you from taking risks that could lead to growth.

Instead, concentrate on what could go right. Visualize your success, set clear and achievable goals, and remind yourself of the reasons you started your side hustle in the first place. Surrounding yourself with positive, like-minded individuals will reinforce this mindset, helping you stay optimistic and resilient in the face of challenges.

Surrounding yourself with like-minded individuals and seeking out support is essential for the success of your side hustle. By joining small business clubs, participating in support groups, learning from successful people, and embracing coaching and encouragement, you can build a strong foundation for growth. Focus on the possibilities of success, and let the inspiration and guidance from those around you fuel your entrepreneurial journey. With the right support system, you'll be better equipped to navigate challenges and achieve your goals, turning your side hustle into a thriving business.

7

Final Thoughts

A s you navigate the journey of building your side hustle or small business, remember that success is often the result of persistence, learning, and adaptability.

Case Studies of More Success Than Failure

When you look at the broader picture, you'll find that many entrepreneurs have achieved success despite numerous obstacles. For every failure, there are countless stories of people who persevered, adapted, and eventually succeeded. By studying these case studies, you can draw inspiration and learn valuable lessons that will help you in your venture. Remember, success often comes to those who are willing to push through challenges and keep moving forward.

Fear Is Not Real Unless You Let It Be

Fear is a natural emotion, but it only has power over you if you let it. Many entrepreneurs experience fear at various stages of their journey, whether it's fear of failure, fear of the unknown, or fear of making the wrong decision. However, it's important to recognize that fear is often a product of our thoughts rather than a reflection of reality. By acknowledging your fears and facing them head-on, you can prevent them from holding you back. Focus on what you can control and take small, courageous steps toward your goals.

Learn From Yourself, Keep a Journal

One of the most effective ways to learn and grow as an entrepreneur is by keeping a journal. Documenting your experiences, thoughts, and feelings allows you to reflect on your journey, identify patterns, and learn from your mistakes and successes. A journal can also serve as a source of motivation, reminding you of how far you've come and the challenges you've overcome. Regularly reviewing your journal can help you stay on track and make informed decisions as you move forward.

Review These Steps Before You Quit

Before you consider giving up on your side hustle, take a moment to review the steps you've taken so far. Reflect on your goals, the challenges you've faced, and the progress you've made. Consider whether there are any adjustments you can make to your approach, such as changing your strategy, seeking support, or redefining your goals. Often, a slight shift in perspective or strategy can make a significant difference, allowing you to overcome obstacles and continue on the path to success.

Be Open to Change and Roll With It

In the ever-evolving world of entrepreneurship, adaptability is the key that will open . Markets change, customer preferences shift, and new challenges arise. To succeed, you must be open to change and willing to adapt your approach as needed. Embrace change as an opportunity for growth rather than a setback. By staying flexible and rolling with the punches, you'll be better equipped to navigate the ups and downs of entrepreneurship and ultimately achieve your goals.

8

Conclusion

Start by identifying what's working well and what areas need improvement. Continuously refine your product or service to meet the evolving needs of your target audience. Build strong relationships with customers through excellent service and engagement, which can lead to positive reviews and repeat business. Utilize effective marketing strategies to increase visibility and attract more clients. Stay organized and manage your time efficiently to balance your side hustle with other responsibilities. Lastly, set realistic goals and monitor your progress, adjusting your strategies as needed to ensure continued growth and success.

Building a successful side hustle or small business is a journey filled with challenges, learning opportunities, and personal growth. By surrounding yourself with supportive, like-minded individuals, staying focused on your goals, and remaining open to change, you can overcome obstacles and turn your vision into reality. Remember that fear is only as real as you allow it to be, and success is within your reach if you persist, adapt, and continue learning. As you move forward, keep this road map in mind, and never underestimate the power of perseverance and a positive mindset. It is the fuel to your destination.

.

.

.

Printed in Great Britain
by Amazon